3 Ways To Reach The Top Of Google

The Quick Way, The Right Way, and The 'Expensive' Way

A comprehensive look at how to attain ranking in local searches, as well as organic placement and pertinent information on PPC advertising.

By Mark Cass

First Print Edition June 2018

Up Your Averages
ISBN-13: 978-0692138977 (Custom Universal)
ISBN-10: 0692138978

Edited by, Tim Jacobs
Jacobs Writing Consultants
Jacobswc.com

Book Cover Design by, Tom Messina
Blue Grey Marketing & Total Concept Inc.
bluegreymarketing.com | TotalConcept.com

Table Of Contents

Dedications

To My Mom and My Uncle Tony *for always believing in me and my writing talent*

Brian Solt *for not seeing any of the reasons why not, and for only seeing the reasons why I could*

John Pesano *for helping me understand SEO*

Tim Jacobs for *inviting me to Master Networks*

Anisity Rowe for *Never, ever giving up on me*

To Myself

Be Encouraged, You're Doing It

#OneInARow

#UpYourAverages

#MeetYouAtTheTop

bluegreymarketing.com

3 Ways To Reach The Top Of Google

The Quick Way, The Right Way, and The 'Expensive' Way

A comprehensive look at how to attain ranking in local searches, as well as organic placement and pertinent information on PPC advertising.

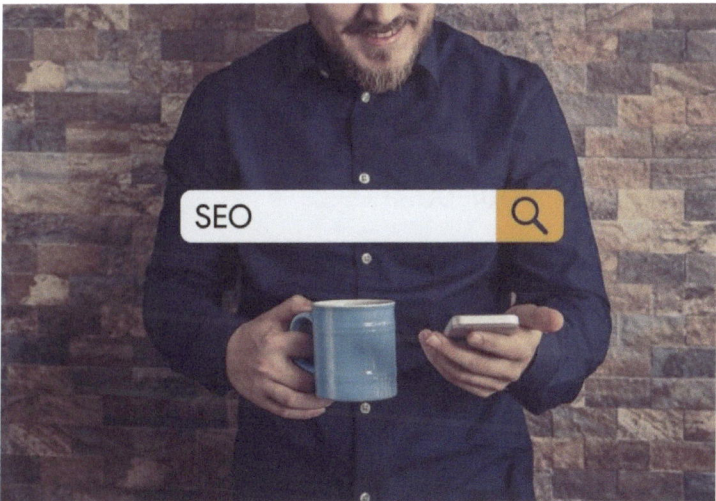

Local SEO –
The Right Way

Laying The Foundation

Let us begin with The Right Way, establishing a solid foundation for your business. All good SEO efforts on the web begin with Local SEO, which is the equivalent of registering your business with Google. Letting Google know who you are, what you do, and where and when you do it.

The first step to registering with Google is by creating or claiming a Google My Business account for your business.

If you have ever done a Google search before and seen the results populate at the top of the page with the map, star ratings, address, and phone number, that is what we are referring to when using the term local SEO.

Usually the top three most relevant businesses or service providers under the key word or phrase that you searched will be displayed, with an option to click to see more.

This display of the top 3 businesses are referred to as the 'Three Pack'.

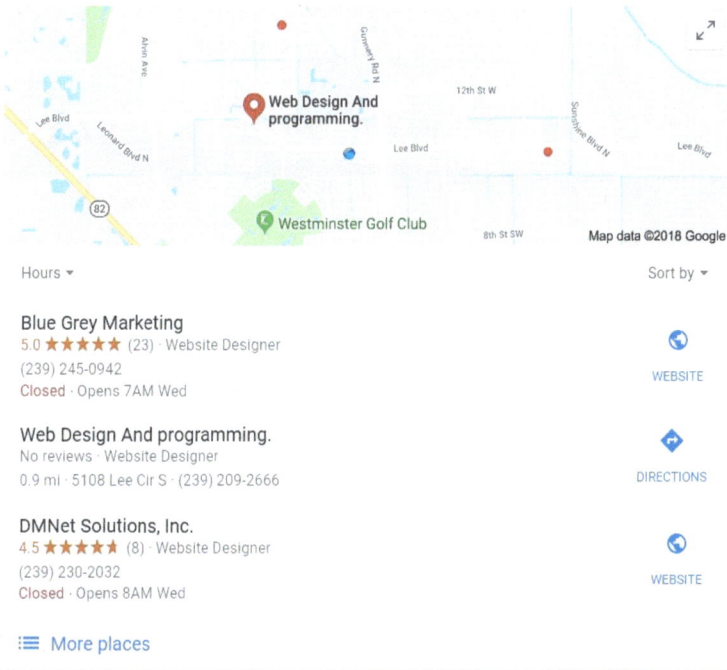

Blue Grey Marketing
5.0 ★★★★★ (23) · Website Designer
(239) 245-0942
Closed · Opens 7AM Wed

Web Design And programming.
No reviews · Website Designer
0.9 mi · 5108 Lee Cir S · (239) 209-2666

DMNet Solutions, Inc.
4.5 ★★★★★ (8) · Website Designer
(239) 230-2032
Closed · Opens 8AM Wed

More places

Depending on the industry, it could very likely be the first result displayed on Google, and that can have a huge impact on the amount of business you do each day, each week, each month and thereby a direct effect on your bottom line.

The First page, or the top of Google, is the

most coveted Digital Real Estate on the entire internet.

When it comes to being found online, the growth of your business will depend on how well your business is to find online.

Local SEO is not only the best place to start. You should consider it to be Required.

Step 1:

Create/Claim Your Google My Business Page

Google My Business

It is free to create a [1]Google My Business page and it shouldn't take more than 20 minutes to complete. This will register your business, hours, phone number, and directions with Google, and enable your business info to appear in Google's Search Results and Google Maps.

Be sure to add pictures of your business and a great description so people can familiarize

---

[1] http://bluegreymarketing.com/2017/10/07/google-my-business-a-guide/

themselves with your business directly from your local Google My Business page. Only a partial setup will be allowed until the business and address are verified by Google.

This process is done by Google manually sending you a postcard with a PIN, so make sure to check your mail! Normal mailing time is 3 to 5 days.

Step 2: Create Business Mentions

Once you have received your PIN from Google, verified your business, and completed your Google My Business profile, you have improved your online profile immensely. However, this is only the beginning. Plenty of work remains.

The next step is to make sure your business is listed, reviewed, and mentioned on other sites across the internet.

Sites such as corporate directories (*Yellow Pages, BBB, Chamber of Commerce*), social media sites (*Facebook, Instagram, Google Plus*), review sites (Yelp!), and location based apps (*Trip Advisor, FourSquare, Waze)* are important).

The more sites you can get reporting your business information to Google, the better!

It's the digital equivalent to word of mouth advertising.

Google is always listening to see which businesses are being talked about the most.

In this case, less is NOT more.

Ideally, one wants their business to be mentioned on at least **50 sites or more**. The bigger your digital footprint, the more relevant Google considers you to be.

This process can be lengthy and tedious if you are starting from scratch, but a good way to get started is to join and creating profiles for your business on all the sites that have clout with Google. This will include, *but not be limited to,* Facebook, Instagram, Google Plus, and any other social media platform relevant to your industry i.e. Pinterest, LinkedIn.

Yelp! is another big one that you want to be on. All of these sites are considered to be highly credible by Google, and having an active profile on them gives your business a higher relevancy score with Google as well.

Since joining and managing all of these sites can be time consuming, laborious, and often times confusing, Blue Grey Marketing has become a leader in the world of digital marketing, offering this very service. We create profiles and manage your business listing on more than 60 different sites across the internet for 12 months at a time.

These sites are a cross section of the type of sites that Google finds credible and relevant to scoring how a business ranks in its algorithm.

They include Directory sites, Review sites, Social Media sites, Smart Phone apps, as well as business listings on all the major search engines.

Or, one can manage all this themselves – if they were so inclined.

A list of suggested sites to join and manage include

2 Find Local, **Bing,** *eLocal, iBegin, 8 Coupons,* **BizWiki, EZlocal,** *iGlobal, AB Local BrownBook.net,*

*Factual, InsiderPages, AirYell, ChamberofCommerce.com, FindOpen, **Kudzu,** AllOnSearch, **CitySearch,** FourSquare, Local.Com, AmericanTowns, CitySquares, GetFave, LocalDatabase, **Apple Maps,** Credibility.com, GetLocal24/7, Local Pages, AroundMe, Cylex, **Google My Business,** Local Stack, Avantar, **DexKnows,** Here, M**apQuest,** My Local Services, The Internet Chamber of Commerce, Hot Frog, n49, Tom Tom, **Yahoo, Merchant Circle,** Navmii, Topix, Talwal, Telenav, Opendi, Tueplo, YaSabe, Yellow Wise, Pointcom, USCity.net, Yellow Moxie, **Yelp!,** Public Reputation, Vote4theBest Yellow Page City, Soleo, **ShowMeLocal, Waze, White & Yellow Pages,** Where To Go, **Superpages***

Step 3: Get reviews

Nothing is better for your business online than positive reviews. Google assigns a lot of weight to businesses that get positive reviews, and even more weight to businesses that take the time to respond to those reviews. Please feel free to check out our blog posts for more detailed information both [2]here and here.

---

[2] http://bluegreymarketing.com/2017/09/01/google-reviews-new-seo/

Besides the obvious relevance of good reviews, they also serve to enhance your "click through rate," an important indicator to Google regarding the relevance of your business. Businesses with the most good reviews or the higher star ratings usually get more clicks; the more clicks, the more relevant to Google.

A good way to begin this endeavor is by coming up with a list of about 50 customers/clients/friends/family; anyone who will leave a positive review about your business. However, you want to be careful not to do this all at one time, as getting 20 or 30 new reviews in a short amount of time may set off red flag alerts with Google.

Pick your people to ask and spread this ask out over a month, or three. The idea would be to stagger your requested reviews out in an organic fashion, so the reviews appear to be coming in naturally.

It is also important to train your staff to ask customers for reviews and develop regular routines of requesting reviews.

Blue Grey Marketing
Lehigh Acres, FL

5.0 ★★★★★ 22 reviews

Sort by: Most relevant ▾

Write a review

👍 Like

Appliance Discount Center
1 review · 1 photo

★★★★★ a month ago

Love the website Blue Grey Marketing made for us. We couldnt believe the day it went live it started generating leads for us. We were so happy, we referred them to two of our other friends the same day. Best web design team in all of Fort Myers.

Shari Haling
3 reviews

★★★★★ 4 months ago

Luv Luv Luv them! They have truly made a huge difference to my business and my life. Anisity was a life saver keeping me on track and not missing a beat with ideas, deadlines and awesome fb flyers for everything!! Mark was great at sending me about changes and tidbits to help increase our reach even with the ever changing algorithms! They truly cared about me, my staff, my guests and Catch 22. Words honestly can't express my gratitude. You guys are THE best!!
Shari - Catch 22 Live Music & Sports Bar

Nicholas Kocolis
1 review

★★★★★ 3 months ago · ⚑

Blue Grey marketing and Mark Cass in particular are without a doubt leaders in the industry. The quality of service and the genuine concern for me and my business is unparalleled in this field. I am very glad to have met and done business with Blue Grey marketing and would consider it my company's great pleasure to continue to work with Blue Grey marketing and Mark Cass many years into the future . We are very thankful for all that he has done and always encourage others to try his service and see the difference that Blue Grey marketing makes in their own company.

Brian Solt
2 reviews

★★★★★ 5 months ago

Mark is a hard worker who takes pride in customer service. He is a connecter promoting customers online and offline. He promotes his clients online through social media/web design and offline through referral networking groups and social mixers. He's a proactive, creative and knowledgable marketer

If you aren't proactively getting reviews, then the only reviews you get will be bad reviews.

Though your Google My Business page is a great place to start, but don't forget

about Yelp, Facebook, Trip Advisor, and the Better Business Bureau either. *You need reviews everywhere.*

The more, the better!

Step 4: Backlinks Improve Your Local SEO - The More, The Better

Another important determining factor on where Google places your business in its local search results is the number of local backlinks that you have.

The more local businesses that are connecting to yours, the stronger your domain authority score.

Which is another important determination in the Google Algorithm and ranking system.

You can think of Domain Authority as a score for your online reputation. Each backlink is a business that is vouching for you, and the more people vouching for you, the stronger your reputation. The stronger Google sees your reputation as, the higher your business will score in its franking algorithm. For a local service oriented business, it is imperative that you create local links pointing back to your site.

You could begin by requesting to be listed on a 'partners section' on as many of your vendors' web sites as possible.

If you have any corporate clients, then you would very much want to see if they would be willing to place a link back to your website on their website.

Chances are, corporate clients or vendors have well established online reputations, and by them linking back to you, your business will inherit the benefit of their well-established credibility.

Another idea is to get involved with a local school or community and sponsor a youth athletics team; in return, they should link back to you on their 'sponsor' page.

All of these types of backlinks are indicators to Google that your business is <u>reputable</u>, <u>relevant</u>, and <u>local</u>.

Step 5: Improve Your On-Site SEO

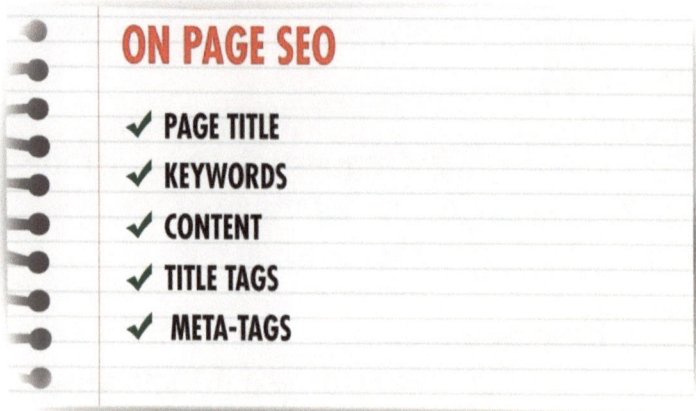

ON PAGE SEO

✔ PAGE TITLE
✔ KEYWORDS
✔ CONTENT
✔ TITLE TAGS
✔ META-TAGS

The fifth step here is actually the first step.

'On-site SEO' has to do with your actual website content, keyword density, and overall optimization.

Unfortunately, a lot of web builders do not understand SEO thoroughly; and they copy and paste the service descriptions provided to them by the business owner and neither one knew how to, or cared to, do keyword research or craft the written content in such a way that it included several relevant search terms or phrases in their homepage text or service pages.

Google is not going to know that Blue Grey Marketing is a digital marketing agency specializing in SEO, Social Media, and Web Design in Fort Myers, Cape Coral, Estero, Naples, and Nationwide unless we have specific pages that say that.

The same is true of you and your business.

If you are a plastic surgeon in Naples, Florida. then this needs to be very clear and apparent on your website.

Good Advice to any business owner building or redesigning a website is to display your business name, address, and phone number 'above the fold' on your website. Make it the first thing that people and Google see when they visit your site.

In the title tag of your site's source code, be sure to reference your local market.

On your contact page, make sure to list out directions to your office and include local landmarks so people can easily find your location. All of your displayed photos/images, should include Alt Text and photo descriptions.

As google cannot see images. As of now Google can only read text, and interpret speech. Iso images must be described in Alt Text.

Your local search results tie back into your website. Therefore, your website needs to be a true local indicator.

Don't go overboard, though; there is no need to mention multiple cities such as Naples, Fort Myers, Cape Coral, or whatever your town cluster is.

Google will consider this to be keyword stuffing and frown upon the practice.

Instead, Google prefers to rank sites that work their location and keywords in naturally.

Google prefers a conversational tone when describing services. If you would like to test your site's SEO score, we provide one on our website bluegreymarketing.com.

You can find a link to our [3]SEO Testing Tool here.

---

[3] http://bluegreymarketing.com/test-your-site/

Open For Business

If you haven't taken the steps above to improve your local SEO, it is the equivalent of having a sign on your front door that says, "We're Closed."

You want to make it known to Google that you are open for business and what kind of business it is you are open for.

If you have a local office and spend 2 hours a week in a smart and efficient manner on your local SEO, you will reap the benefits for years to come.

Don't be discouraged if your business isn't ranking in the top three results within a week, though. Like anything in life, Google placement must be earned.

It can sometimes take quite a bit of time and consistent strides of improvement before Google rewards your efforts.

Other times, not so much. A lot of this is also determined by the strength of your competitors' SEO – *but that's another book.*

AdWords -
The Quick Way

Why Your Business Needs AdWords

Google reserves the top part of its online real estate for those willing to outbid their competitor for it. This advertising platform is where Google generates *80%* of all their revenue from.The basic workings of it go like this – a business owner creates an ad that contains two headlines as well as a URL address, and dictates to Google which keywords they want their ad to appear for.

Then when people perform search queries on Google, their ad will theoretically appear at one of the top positions on the page.

How often and how well this process works depends on a lot of different factors, too many to mention here. For now, we are focused more on the 'Whys' of AdWords than we are the Hows.

Why # 1
AdWords Are Faster Than SEO
Another of the key factors in Googles Ranking Algorithm is the length of time your website has been up.

Usually, the longer the better. A website with seniority, so to speak develops a kind of authority and credibility not just with Google but many other online references and mentions as well. These factors weigh heavily in Google's algorithm.

This can pose quite the problem for new business websites – or even old business websites that have recently changed their URL or web domain name.

AdWords goes a long way in helping to make up this difference.

With the creation of an ad, and a designated ad budget, your business can be listed at the top of the first page of Google, under the keywords pertaining to your business and its services, in the local area you perform them in **Instantaneously**!

In theory anyway.

AdWords can provide a big advantage for a small business trying to compete with big businesses in their area.

Though AdWords can be very powerful, one should not rely on Pay-Per-Click (PPC) advertising alone.

PPC should only be used as a complement to your marketing strategy, *not as the marketing strategy in its entirety.*

Still not convinced? Here are a few more answered 'whys' as to why it's to your advantage to be using AdWords to grow your business.

Why # 2
AdWords Are Scalable

It's very difficult to find methods of marketing that are scalable – meaning it's difficult to continuously find ways to generate leads that *do not require more effort in order to generate more leads.*

Thus, another reason for the rise in popularity of Google AdWords.

The AdWords platform is highly scalable, which is why so many companies across the globe are spending millions each year on Google AdWords Pay-Per-Click advertising.

As a result of well-managed PPC campaigns, there are businesses experiencing tremendous growth, with a large increase in sales that are directly linked back to their AdWords campaign.

This makes AdWords a highly effective choice for businesses that need to generate a lot of leads very quickly, but have limited resources.

Why #3
AdWords Are Measurable

AdWords is one of the most measurable

marketing techniques in existence.

Unlike magazines, billboards, or television, AdWords is very transparent, and provides a plethora of information regarding PPC metrics, really allowing you to see at a granular level what is working and what isn't.

With metrics like this, you can tell pretty quickly if your campaign is running efficiently or not.

Why #4
AdWords Are Flexible

AdWords gives you many customization options, so you set up and adjust your ad campaigns to specifically meet your need, i.e. get more website traffic, get more phone calls, app downloads, etc.

For Example

- Specify keyword match types – You can, for example, have Google only display your ad to people who search for an exact keyword you specify, like "Digital Marketing Services in Naples, FL" – filtering out traffic on general terms related to marketing or online advertising.

- Use ad extensions to have Google display your product images, your phone number, your physical location, or even a set of different website links – you can even initiate a chat or get an email address right from the Search Engine Results Pages (SERP).

- Target your audience by their location, the time of day, user language, browser or device type, and more.

AdWords puts you in control and lets you decide where, when, and to whom your ads are displayed.

Why #6
Paid Traffic Converts Better Than Organic Traffic

No doubt that Organic SEO is what we all want. However, evidence does exist that suggests [4]paid search traffic converts better

---

[4] https://moz.com/ugc/true-or-false-organic-traffic-converts-better-than-ppc

[than organic traffic](#) with conversion rates up to two times higher.

Think about it – most Pay-Per-Click campaigns are keyword driven and written to appear to people already in the buying cycle.

Why wouldn't that strategy convert more traffic than people just finding your site by accident?
There are a lot of reasons for businesses to utilize the power of AdWords.

A lot of sales and growth can take place as a result of using the Google AdWords platform.

When the campaign is optimized and well managed; but when it is not, a small business can go broke trying to learn and fumble their way through a Pay-Per-Click campaign.

It's a lot like learning to play poker; most people lose a lot before they ever win any.

That's why Blue Grey Marketing has the very

best in trained staff that are not only AdWords certified but renew their certification routinely.

We excel in the area of Google AdWords and PPC advertising and are always available for a discussion about whether or not AdWords is right for your business.

Organic SEO

The 'Expensive' Way

There are different methods to get to the top of Google and this is the one that I chose to refer to as The 'Expensive' Way. Because this is the one that usually requires a heavier investment than the other methods, but in no way is it expensive when compared to its Lifelong value. Just consider for a moment, the business you are losing by not being at the top of Googles search results.

Everyone knows that LOCATION IS EVERYTHING and the front page of Google is 'Prime Digital Real Estate'.

Very rarely will someone wander past the first or second page of online search results searching for a service provider.

So if you are not on the first page, you don't exist!

The previous two chapters of this book dealt with getting your business registered on Google and taking the necessary steps to be recognized by Google and making sure your business shows up in Googles Local Listings as well as buying position and ranking on Google via [5]AdWords.

This chapter deals with the Holy Grail of all SEO efforts.

Organic Search Engine Optimization or SEO for short, is the act of optimizing a website to be more search engine friendly.

---

[5] https://bluegreymarketing.com/2017/10/29/quick-way-adwords/

It involves a wide range of factors, starting with keyword optimization and link building, and includes a great deal of website optimization as well – this is referred to as 'onsite optimization'.

A good job usually requires extensive set up, and fairly routine maintenance after set up is completed.

Google uses a complex set of algorithms to rank websites, and tweaks and changes happen often. So, using what is known as 'Black Hat' tactics (cheating) eventually comes to light, and when Google responds, you are usually banished to the 4th or 5th page - never to be considered relevant again.

However, when you build out your SEO campaigns the right way then you will naturally begin to rise up through Googles ranking algorithm and you never have to pay Google anything.

Though organic SEO services are quite laborious in initial set up, once you have a campaign up and running, it then becomes fairly inexpensive to manage monthly from there on out.

So over time, having your business rank well on Google becomes an inexpensively maintained stream of revenue.

This is why everyone's goal is for their business to be listed at or near the top of the first page of Google.

The following is a list compiled by [6]Forbes, detailing seven specific reasons why your business should seriously consider making an investment into your organic SEO strategy:

- **SEO Works** – Point Blank Period! The key is focusing on creating or improving your optimal user experience while still adhering to

---

6

https://www.forbes.com/forbes/welcome/?toURL=https://www.forbes.com/business/&refURL=&referrer=

sound SEO strategies. The more you do this, the more your business will be rewarded with higher positioning and organic traffic.

- **It is not going to stop working any time soon** – The basic way search engines operate dictates that employing sound SEO principles and strategies will remain rewarding for years and years to come. Even with the advent of search engines being utilized by audio and video now, their basic principle of searching by keywords will remain the same.

- **It is cost-effective**– When you compare the costs of maintaining a consistent organic SEO strategy against the cost of maintaining a PPC or Social Media Marketing strategy, the costs are fairly nominal. This point is underscored even more when you consider that you quit getting results with the other methods when you quit paying for them.

Your organic SEO strategies will remain a bedrock foundation of all your marketing strategies once set up and an established routine created for maintenance. *No further monetary investment required.*

Gains made organically have a tendency to be longer lasting – even without continued maintenance just like most things when they are done correctly.

Over time, organic SEO has statistically, always yielded a much higher return on investment than any other form of popular online marketing/advertising.

- **Search engines are grabbing more market share** – More than 80% of all online shoppers today now check online reviews before making a purchase, and this number is steadily rising. Without a strategic Search

Engine Marketing plan, your business will have a very hard time becoming, relevant with all the websites out there competing for the same dollar you are competing for.

- **Rise of mobile bandwidth and local search optimization–** The amount of web traffic that emanates from mobile devices now exceeds the amount coming from desktop computers.

The dramatic explosion of cell phone internet usage has changed the way people search, and this is why your local SEO cannot be neglected either.

- **Not having an active and up to date online profile is a liability** – With all the algorithm tweaks, changes, and updates that Google makes the way they view websites has dramatically changed over the years.

   Things that never existed before, such as social media indicators, are now given a considerable amount of weight, and have the potential to be a difference maker when Google is deciding which businesses make its First page and which ones do not.

Another indicator of an poorly ranking site is its mobile responsiveness, or lack thereof.

Google gives ranking preference to websites that have been optimized for mobile and are responsive to whatever screen they are viewed on, whether that be a desktop, tablet, or smartphone.

Google provides a free [7]mobile responsive testing site. If you'd like to test yours.

To see if your site is responsive or not, just enter your URL and hit submit.
As with most things in life paying attention to your SEO once is not enough. Your online strategy needs to include routine updates and online profile maintenance each week. The longer you employ this practice, the stronger your SEO foundation and

[7] https://search.google.com/test/mobile-friendly

reputation becomes. Therefore the more Google regards you as being relevant.

So, the best time to start your SEO strategy was several years ago. The second best time to do so is today!

- **Your competitors are doing it–** Jason Bayless, the owner of a website that tracks and ranks the efficacy and service of many of the nation's top SEO companies, says

"Remember, SEO is a never-ending process. If you are not moving forward and improving your position, then you are losing ground to a competitor who is."

Put another way – while you've been busy slipping, your competitor's been busy gripping.

It's time to stop the slide!

The importance of implementing an organic SEO strategy sooner rather than later simply cannot be overstated, and although the investment might be front loaded, in the larger scope of things

- Organic SEO is a lot cheaper to invest in than its SEO counterparts.

- It attracts more click-throughs than paid ad campaigns.
- Organic search results are more trusted than Pay-Per-Click advertising.

Our recommendation: Implement, and implement sooner rather than later.

If you'd like a free consultation to discuss your SEO options and a sound marketing strategy for your business then please [8]Contact Us.

---

[8] https://bluegreymarketing.com/reach-us/

Bonus Chapter (1)

Google My Business
What Is It?

Google My Business is an easy-to-set-up dashboard where small business owners can manage their presence on Google's search engine.

When someone searches for local services on Google, information related to local businesses such as a phone number, an address, their reviews, a website link, etc., are pulled from their verified [9]Google My Business page and populated in the search results.

Kind of like a library's card catalog system, where each card contains an individual's business location and service information.

If you don't set up an account and register with Google, then Google cannot provide your businesses information to individuals searching for your services.

---

[9]

https://www.google.com/search?rlz=1C1VFKB_enUS633US633&q=Blue+Grey+Marketing+400+Harry+Ave+N.+Lehigh+Acres+maps&oq=Blue+Grey+Marketing+400+Harry+Ave+N.+Lehigh+Acres+maps&gs_l=psy-ab.3...12362.17752.0.18264.6.6.0.0.0.0.250.748.0j3j1.4.0....0...1.1.64.psy-ab..2.3.589...35i39k1j33i160k1.0.BMwAIOWlKdM

Google My Business was formerly known as Google Places, and more recently Google Maps. In recent years Google has changed its format into what is now known as Google My Business.

As such, it has become an influential factor in determining the ranking of business on Google as well as all the other Search Engines.

A completely filled out, current, and regularly maintained Google My Business account is of paramount importance to a business trying to get noticed online and generate more sales.

Google My Business not only sends traffic to your website but through your front door as well.

That's why the importance of regularly maintaining your Google My Business account CAN NOT be overstated. We recommend giving this at least 2 hours of your time a week. Pick a day and a time and be consistent and purposeful when responding to reviews as well as with your updates, photos, and posts.

Gone are the days when simply having once created a Google My Business profile was adequate.

Your businesses Google profile (Google My Business) should be managed and thought of like a social media account. A social media account that you are active on.

How Google Determines Local Ranking *(straight from Google)*

[10][According to Google,](#) Local Search Results are based on 3 things Primary Factors:

---

[10] https://support.google.com/business/answer/7091?hl=en

- **Relevance**
  Refers to how well a local listing matches what someone is searching for.

  Adding complete and detailed information about your business will help Google better understand your business and match your listing with all relevant search inquiries.

- **Distance**
  This factor takes into account how far each potential search result is from the location of the search term at the time it is being searched for.

  In other words, Google determines where you are when searching, and desires to provide search results relevant to your proximity.

  In the instance that a user doesn't specify location information in their search, Google will calculate distance based on what's known about their location.

- **Prominence**

  Refers to how well-known a business is.

  Some places are more prominent in the offline world; this same prominence is often reflected in local search results as well. For example, famous museums, landmark hotels, or well-known store brands that are familiar to many people are also likely to be prominent in local search results.

  Prominence is ALSO based on other information that Google has about a business from across the web such as local citations, directory listings, social media profiles, blog articles, and of course, other Google products themselves i.e. Google Plus and YouTube.

Reviews are another giant factor in your Prominence score.

The number of reviews your business has on Google is important, but so is the number of reviews you have on Yelp, Trip Advisor, Facebook and any other place that you can leave reviews on the internet.

Another important factor regarding Reviews and online Prominence is *Responding To Them*.

Google likes it a whole lot when you do respond. Not so much when you don't.

Google averages your score from these 3 factors for all of the businesses in your area that meet the requested search criteria to help find the most relevant search results. The more relevant you are, the higher you will rank.

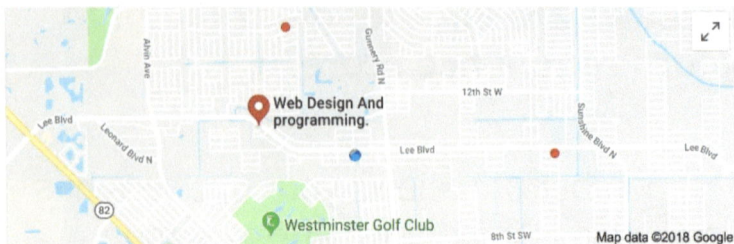

Hours ▾   Sort by ▾

Blue Grey Marketing
5.0 ★★★★★ (23) · Website Designer
(239) 245-0942
Closed · Opens 7AM Wed

🌐
WEBSITE

Web Design And programming.
No reviews · Website Designer
0.9 mi · 5108 Lee Cir S · (239) 209-2666

🔷
DIRECTIONS

DMNet Solutions, Inc.
4.5 ★★★★★ (8) · Website Designer
(239) 230-2032
Closed · Opens 8AM Wed

🌐
WEBSITE

☰ More places

For Example

Googles algorithm might decide that a business farther away from a searchers location is more likely to have what they're looking for than a business that's closer and therefore rank it higher in the local search results, or vice versa.

Google My Business Posts: What Are They and Why Do I Care?

Once you're logged into your Google My

48

Business account and are looking at your dashboard, look on the left side of the screen. You will see 'Posts.'

From there, you'll have the option to add a new a wide variety of new posts. A few of the ways that Google has introduced so far—ways that businesses can use these new business posts—are:

- Announcing new promotions or daily specials.

- Promoting visibility of new and upcoming events.

- Highlighting some of your newest products or feature best-sellers.

- Taking reservations, attracting signups for a newsletter, or selling products directly.

Upon deciding to create your post, you'll encounter several options. You can use any or all of them to complete your post.

A few options are the abilities to add an image, a title, and up to 300 words of text.

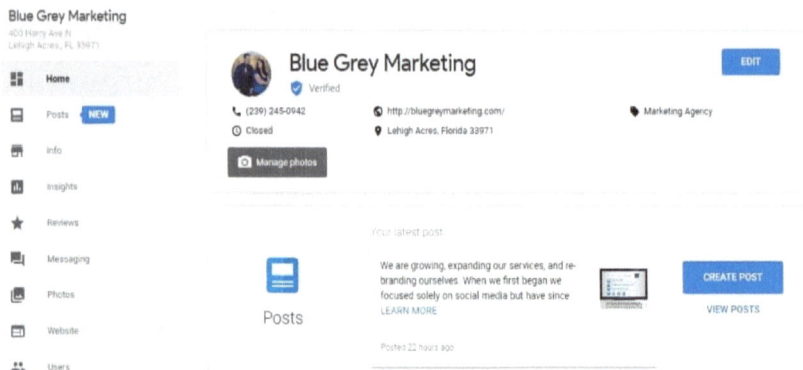

This is best utilized when you use the allotted space of 300 words to announce your service or special and use as many different keywords as possible, as these posts are searchable and become immediately eligible for inclusions in Googles SERPs (Search Engine Result Pages).

You can also add a call-to-action button with a variety of different options, including 'learn more,' 'reserve,' 'buy,' 'sign up,' or 'get offer'.

A Few Need to Knows

Listed below are a few of the best practices to employ when creating Google My Business posts either for ourselves or for clients:

- **Do not use sales-y or overly promotional language.** [11]Google explicitly forbids the use of gimmicky type language, such as "BOGO 75% off!" These posts aren't the place to spam advertisements; they will be removed by Google.

   Instead, use these posts as an opportunity to organically inform your customers and other internet browsers about the latest happenings in your business, the same way you would in a blog or a social media post.

---

[11]

https://support.google.com/business/answer/7390603?hl=en&ref_to pic=7343035

51

- **Include as much information as possible for each Post.**

  Google gives you multiple fields to fill out, so try to fill out all of them.

  Visible, catchy, concise headlines usually attract the most attention, and a bright, well-focused image will also help your post to stand out.

  You'll also want to include plenty of descriptive content as well. The more the better (up to 300 words). Google doesn't give the exact word count out specifically, but it's probable that this is the information it uses to determine the relevance of your post in its various keyword queries.

- **Be timely and personal**
  Google gives preferential treatment to businesses that use Google My Business posts as ways to advertise time-sensitive information, such as temporary offers, upcoming events, or seasonal specials. You can edit or

delete your posts at any time.

It's also a good idea to be as personal as possible, appealing to local audiences with small business charm.

Creating A Google My Business Page

The first step is to determine if you need to claim an existing Google My Business page or create a new one from scratch.

So, if you have not done so already, a quick search on [12]Google Maps and [13]Google Search should be enough to determine this.

If you see an existing listing, simply click 'claim this listing' and follow the listed instructions.

If you have no page, then sign into your

---

[12] https://www.google.com/maps/@26.6194759,-81.718525,15z
[13] https://www.google.com

Google Account. From there, you can easily create a new Google My Business page, or just click [14]here.

You will need to get your profile as near completed status as possible, but until you have verified your listing, you will not be able to fully complete your set up.

Google My Business Checklist
- Make sure to correctly fill out all relevant business contact info (*exactly as they are on your website*).
- Add the correct categories to your business.
- Add a profile picture and header photo.
- Complete the "about your business" section.

This should take your profile to about 80%

---

[14] https://www.google.com/business/?gmbsrc=us-en-et-gs-z-gmb-l-z-h~my%7Credirect%7Cu&ppsrc=GMBLR&utm_campaign=us-en-et-gs-z-gmb-l-z-h~my%7Credirect%7Cu&utm_source=gmb&utm_medium=et

complete, which is as far as you can go until you have verified your business with Google.

Verify Your Business

Most Google My Business accounts has to be verified by the U.S. Postal Service rather than by telephone. A few exceptions exist and if it's you. Google will inform you but just assume that your business must verify just like every other business has to verify via US Mail.

At the top of your My Business Page, click on the blue button that says 'Verify Your Business'. Check the details, and Google will then send you a pin code in the mail.

The verification process can take up to two weeks to arrive by mail but usually occurs within 4 to 5 days.

Once you have received your postcard, all that's left to do is to log into your Google

My Business account and enter the pin code. To show that your account is verified Google will display a little check mark beside business name. Once your account is verified, it will start showing in the results for both Google Maps and Google Search.

Updated Posts

An out-of-date Google My Business is a page can often be a liability, as there is often nothing more disappointing than looking at a company before you buy from them and realizing that they have not updated their profile for months, maybe even years. It leaves potential customers not feeling very comfortable and often wondering if you are even still open.

You should update your Google My

Business page at least once a week with both photos and written content. Your latest blogs, customer feedback, news, special offers, and information about you and your business often make great posts for your Google My Business page.

Be sure to include and update photos and videos often (weekly) for best results. People love content, and so do potential customers. When it comes to choosing your business over your competitor's business, you have to find a way to stand out. Properly managing your Google My Business page is a great place to start.

Customer Reviews

[15]Customer reviews are the new SEO, but not just any reviews - responded to reviews. The good ones, the OK ones, and yes, even the bad ones.

The more you respond to your reviews, the

---

[15] https://bluegreymarketing.com/2017/09/01/google-reviews-new-seo/

more favor you gain with Google. This one step alone will place you higher than most of your competitors in local SEO, as they are unaware of what you are reading right now.

The more reviews you have, the more trustworthy your business appears online, and the higher you rank on local search results for your services.

They also serve to reinforce to new customers that your business is worth using, and you will also get a little star rating underneath your business listing. When you are competing with many other competitors, this can help you stand out from the crowd.

Local Citations

Citations are 'mentions' of your business name, address, and sometimes other contact details on other web pages that are not your own.

Sites like Yelp, Yellow Pages, Trip Advisor, etc. serve as good examples of well-known citation sites, and they are a key element of ranking algorithms for both Google and Bing.

If you have quite a few citations online, your business page has a better chance to rank, especially if you are taking care of all the other elements we mentioned as well.

It is better to aim for high-quality sites and always make sure the address you use across the internet is exactly the same, as it needs to be exact and consistent in order to get the most from it.

Have More Questions About Google My Business?

Please do not hesitate to [16]contact us here at Blue Grey Marketing. Our consultations are Free.

---

[16] https://bluegreymarketing.com/reach-us/

Bonus Chapter (2) Of Particular Interest To Restaurants

Restaurants Can Now Edit Their Menu Items With Google My Business

Google My Business has rolled out a new [17]feature specifically for restaurants. Now, owners may manage their GMB accounts themselves, or they can have professionals such as Blue Grey Marketing handling it for them.

Either way, account managers can now create and edit menus to be displayed in their GMB listing.

This new feature can be found from inside the Google My Business dashboard, under the Info tab.

With this new editor, you can now add and edit menu titles, descriptions, and prices for each of your menu items. You can also now further customize menus by separating your menu items into sections such as

Appetizers | Entrees | Desserts

---

[17] https://www.en.advertisercommunity.com/t5/News-Updates/Launch-Menus-Now-Editable-in-GMB-Web/td-p/1627781#

This is quite a bit different than only having the ability to create and edit structured menus via the Google My Business API or third-party menu services, as was the case prior to this new update.

This is another example of Google's never ending quest to display only the most relevant search results.

If you are a restaurant owner or manager and would like to know more about this or just making your establishment more visible on the internet, then please do not hesitate to contact us and schedule a complimentary brainstorming session. [18]bluegreymarketing.com

---

[18] http://bluegreymarketing.com/

A Lesson In What Not To Do

A Law Firm Loses All But One Google Review

Incentivizing individual Google reviews or soliciting Google reviews in bulk is usually, always a bad idea

Reviews make the difference in your online reputation.

Savvy online users are also aware of how much reviews affect your ranking on Google's Search Engine Results Pages.

Evidently, the law firm of Winton & Hiestand, located in Louisville, Kentucky, felt these reviews were important too; so much so that they were offering free family passes to the local zoo in exchange for a 5-Star Review Rating.

They racked up nearly 100 reviews on Google (and more than 1,000 on facebook) before their incentive strategy was [19]reported inside of a Google My

---

19

https://www.en.advertisercommunity.com/t5/forums/v3_1/forumtop icpage/board-id/Spam_and_Policy/page/1/thread-id/22628

Business forum.

Once Google became aware of their policy, they removed every one of their reviews except *one*.

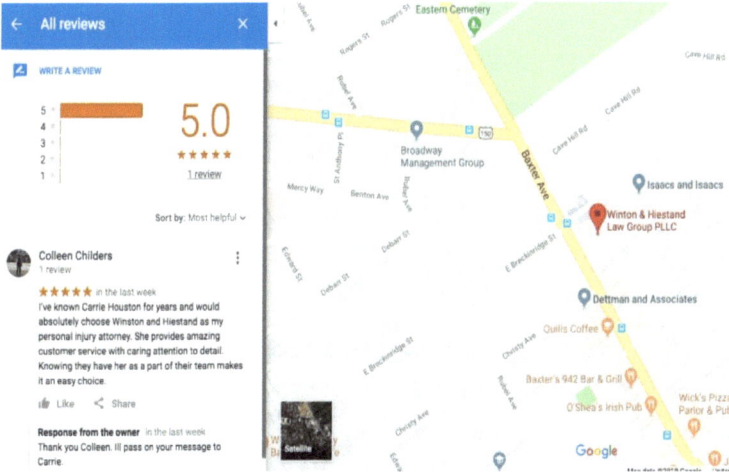

This screen shot was taken Right after all of their reviews were stripped, save this one.

These types of practices are specifically against [20]Google's stated policy regarding written reviews and financial incentive.
In a nutshell, DON'T DO IT.

---

[20]
https://support.google.com/contributionpolicy/answer/7411351?hl=en-GB

These types of reviews, as well as the ones requested in bulk, are both frowned upon on Google and once discovered, can work to your business' disadvantage.

Above and beyond these particular Google policies, there are state laws and federal regulations (FTC rules against "consumer deception") that may be broken by improper review solicitation.

It seems, being a law firm, that they would know this – but alas, a quick review of their [21]Google My Business listing shows they now have 46 new reviews, all occurring in the last week, from many accounts that have never left a review before. Can anyone say "suspicious?"

It will be curious to see how Google will handle their obvious second attempt at gathering reviews in bulk. Obtaining quality reviews is of paramount importance if you want your business to be seen and given

---

[21]

https://www.google.com/search?q=Winton+%26+Hiestand+law+grou p+louisville+ky&oq=Winton+%26+Hiestand+law+group+louisville+ky& aqs=chrome..69i57.15906j0j7&sourceid=chrome&ie=UTF-8#lrd=0x8869718a65086583:0xf976aeb8233aa82c,1,,,

due consideration online.

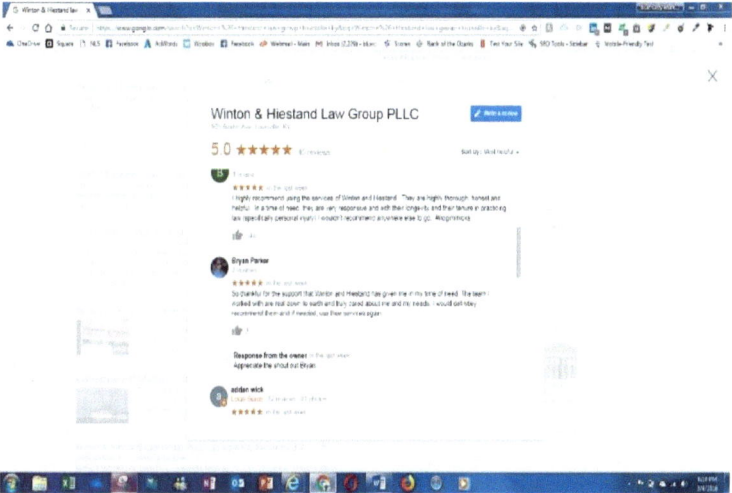

Law firm loses all of their google reviews but one and a week later regain 46 new ones

²²Mark's Bio

Mark has been involved in one entrepreneurial venture or another since adolescence, but he most recently found success as the owner and operator of Metal Recycling and Salvage, founded in 2007.

In this venture, his marketing skills were put to the test almost daily, as he had to find new ways to stand out from so many other competitors at the time, just to survive. It was in this intensely pressurized arena that Mark found ways to not just survive, but thrive,

[22] https://bluegreymarketing.com/reach-us/#1515295138851-47f2ba5f-9835

outlasting many other fly by night ventures and rising to a level of prominence within the scrap metal and recycling industry. Shortly after this, Mark would put his marketing skills on display again as he moved into a corner office located in Downtown Fort Myers, and with just one client, began Effective Marketing Solutions. This venture did not turn out quite as well as he had hoped. What Mark lost in financial success, though, was more than made up for in growth, knowledge, and experience. In 2015, he teamed up with Anisity Rowe to form Blue Grey Marketing, and here they are today, serving the needs of entrepreneurs and business owners everywhere.

Feel free to contact Mark at UpYourAverages@gmail.com for workshops, business coaching, or keynote speaking.

MARK CASS

#Up Your Averages